# Safety

## Karen Durrie

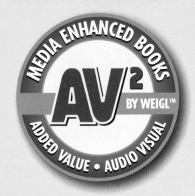

# MEDIA ENHANCED BOOKS
## AV²
### BY WEIGL™
ADDED VALUE • AUDIO VISUAL

Go to **www.av2books.com**, and enter this book's unique code.

## BOOK CODE

**U983120**

**AV² by Weigl** brings you media enhanced books that support active learning.

AV² provides enriched content that supplements and complements this book. Weigl's AV² books strive to create inspired learning and engage young minds in a total learning experience.

# Your AV² Media Enhanced books come alive with...

**Audio**
Listen to sections of the book read aloud.

**Video**
Watch informative video clips.

**Embedded Weblinks**
Gain additional information for research.

**Try This!**
Complete activities and hands-on experiments.

**Key Words**
Study vocabulary, and complete a matching word activity.

**Quizzes**
Test your knowledge.

**Slide Show**
View images and captions, and prepare a presentation.

# ... and much, much more!

Published by AV² by Weigl
350 5th Avenue, 59th Floor  New York, NY  10118
Website: www.av2books.com          www.weigl.com

Library of Congress Cataloging-in-Publicataion Data available upon request.
Fax 1-866-44-WEIGL for the attention of the Publishing Records department.

ISBN 978-1-61690-951-2 (hard cover)

Printed in the United States of America in North Mankato, Minnesota
1 2 3 4 5 6 7 8 9 0  15 14 13 12 11

062011
WEP030611

Project Coordinator: Karen Durrie  Art Director: Terry Paulhus

Weigl acknowledges Getty Images as the primary image supplier for this title.

# Safety

## CONTENTS

3

Workers in our community help keep us safe.

4

**Police Officer**

**Security Guard**

**Paramedic**

**Crossing Guard**

**Lifeguard**

**Forest Ranger**

**Firefighter**

**Health Inspector**

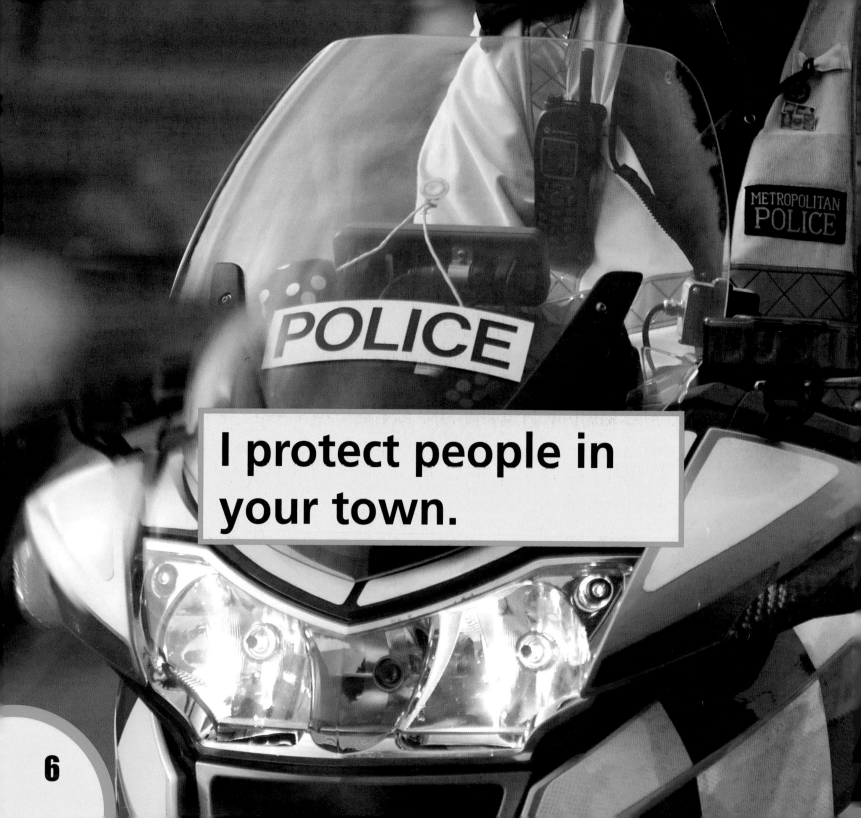

I protect people in your town.

I am a
police officer.

I come fast to help
if you are hurt.

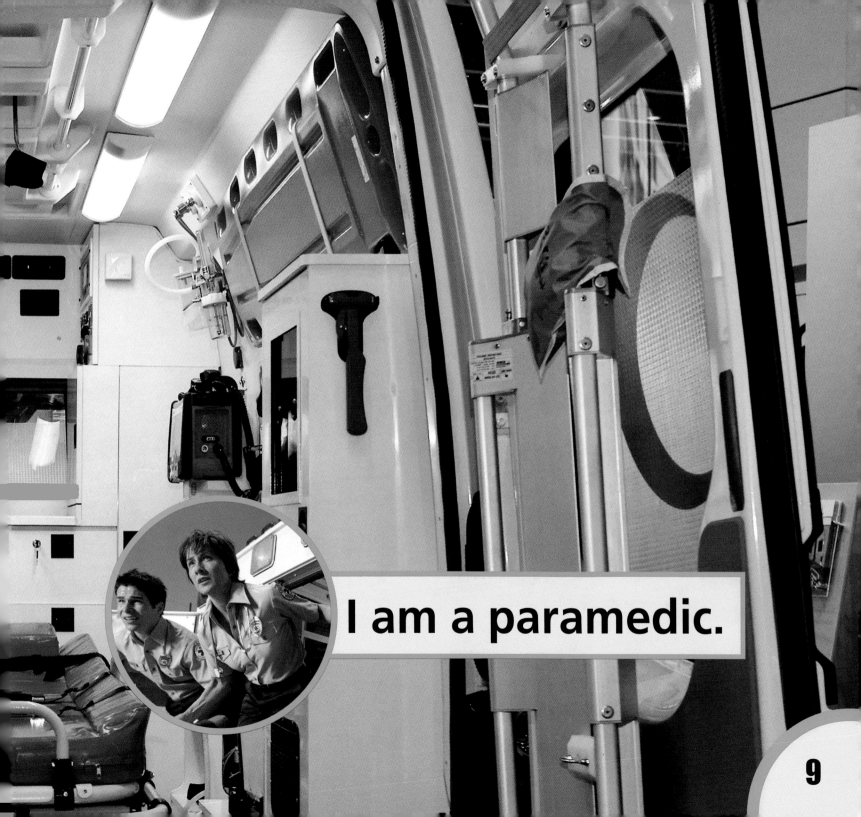

I am a paramedic.

I watch you at the pool and the beach.

I am a lifeguard.

I get you safely across the street.

I am a crossing guard.

I keep watch in buildings, stores, and parks.

I am a
security guard.

I put out fires. I save people and their pets.

I am a firefighter.

I look after the forest and help if you are lost.

18

I am a forest ranger.

I make sure your food is safe to eat.

I am a health inspector.

# SAFETY FACTS

People with common interests can form a community. Many people play roles in keeping a community safe. Read below to learn more about these important workers and the different things they do to keep us safe.

**Safety is the state of being free from danger or injury and feeling secure.** When we feel safe, we feel free to move about our communities comfortably.

**Police officers do many things to protect the communities where they work, and to enforce laws.** Police may patrol in cars, on bicycles, on motorcycles, on foot, or even on horses. They look for violations of the law, hand out tickets to law-breakers, investigate crimes, and arrive quickly in an emergency. They also talk to the public about being safe in the community.

**Paramedics are also called emergency medical service, or EMS.** Paramedics respond to emergency calls when people are hurt and give medical treatment at the scene of accidents. If needed, they transport patients to hospitals and keep up medical treatment en route.

**Lifeguards watch swimmers at lakes, oceans, and swimming pools.** Their job is to observe many people at once and ensure everyone is safe. Lifeguards sit on tall chairs to get a good view of swimmers. They must be expert swimmers and certified in First Aid. They rescue people in trouble and ensure people follow rules.

**Crossing guards work near schools and on busy roadways to help pedestrians cross the street safely.** They wear bright vests or jackets to be easily seen and use signs to stop or direct traffic. Some communities have safety patrols to help schoolchildren cross the street.

**Security guards are used in many places.** They may be hired to protect people or property. They help prevent theft from stores. Some security guards keep watch at parks or special events for signs of crime or disorder. Some also watch TV monitors in special offices to see what is going on in a large area. Security guards also work at airports to ensure passengers travel safely.

**Firefighters do more than put out fires.** They also respond to emergencies such as car accidents. Firefighters are trained to treat people who are hurt or sick, at fires or in other situations. Inspecting buildings to make sure fire safety laws are followed is another part of a firefighter's job.

**Park rangers have many duties.** They help park visitors by providing tours and information, or assistance if people become lost or hurt. Park rangers protect parks by enforcing safety codes for people who hike, climb, ski, boat, camp, fish, or picnic in the park.

**Health inspectors do many things to look after public health and safety.** They inspect places that handle and prepare food, such as restaurants and supermarkets. Health inspectors also work to make sure our drinking water is clean and safe, as well as the water we use for swimming and other recreational activities. Testing air quality in buildings is also part of a health inspector's duties.

# WORD LIST

Research has shown that as much as 65 percent of all written material published in English is made up of 300 words. These 300 words cannot be taught using pictures or learned by sounding them out. They must be recognized by sight. This book contains 27 common sight words to help young readers improve their reading fluency and comprehension. This book also teaches young readers several important content words, such as proper nouns. These words are paired with pictures to aid in learning and improve understanding.

| Page | Sight Words First Appearance |
|------|------------------------------|
| 4 | help, in, keep, our |
| 6 | I, people, your |
| 7 | a |
| 8 | are, come, if, to, you |
| 10 | and, at, the, watch |
| 12 | get |
| 16 | out, put, their |
| 18 | after, look |
| 20 | eat, food, is, make |

| Page | Content Words First Appearance |
|------|--------------------------------|
| 4 | community, workers |
| 5 | crossing, firefighter, forest, guard, health, inspector, lifeguard, officer, paramedic, police, ranger, security |
| 6 | town |
| 10 | beach, pool |
| 12 | street |
| 14 | buildings, parks, stores |
| 16 | fires, pets |

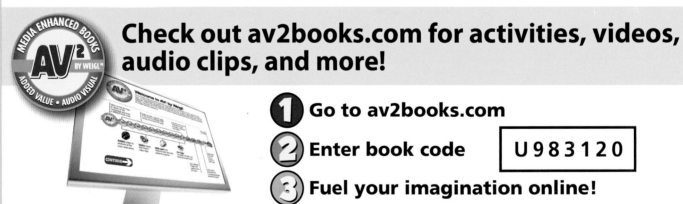